16.95

LIAR, JONES

MAGGIE HANNAN

Liar, Jones

BLOODAXE BOOKS

Copyright © Maggie Hannan 1995

ISBN: 1 85224 308 2

First published 1995 by
Bloodaxe Books Ltd,
P.O. Box 1SN,
Newcastle upon Tyne NE99 1SN.

Bloodaxe Books Ltd acknowledges
the financial assistance of Northern Arts.

Cover printing by J. Thomson Colour Printers Ltd, Glasgow.

Printed in Great Britain by
Bell & Bain Limited, Glasgow, Scotland.

For Ann

Acknowledgements

Acknowledgements are due to the editors of the following publications in which some of these poems first appeared: *Bête Noire, The Gregory Anthology* (Hutchinson, 1990), *The New Lake Poets* (Bloodaxe Books, 1991), *The New Poetry* (Bloodaxe Books, 1993), *Poetry with an Edge* (Bloodaxe Books, new edition, 1993), and *Staple*. Some of the poems were broadcast on *New Voices* (BBC Radio 3), *Stanza* and *Kaleidoscope* (BBC Radio 4).

Maggie Hannan wishes to thank the Society of Authors for an Eric Gregory Award in 1990, and Yorkshire Arts for a writer's bursary which enabled her to complete this book.

Contents

Aubrey, Boris, Christopher. Christ

> *Constitutional psychology seeks a basic taxonomy of human beings.*
> *It asks for a frame of reference against which individuality may be*
> *set off and classified and scaled...the complexity of human beings*
> *makes it advisable to subdivide the problem in such a way that*
> *separate attacks may be made on different levels...*
>
> W.H. SHELDON & S.S. STEVENS
> The Varieties of Temperament

I *Viscerotonic*

Julia was not pleased,
Aubrey, when walrus you

and she touched bottom,
did it, did coition. Well

jellied and of rounded nature,
you're opinionated, not.

Electrocution barely reads,
but yell, you will, and loud.

Viscerotonic and *moronophile*.
Make that loved, forgiven, fat.

II *Somatotonic*

Think Superman, think
Smilin' Jack – those eyes

set NNE and NNW from tip
of chin. He's Viking

King. Has happy knack
of crack – but thick,

and slick as tar. Muscular.
When Boris sleeps, he sleeps

on floors. He snores.
Tough, aggressive. Prat.

III *Cerebrotonic*

God-shy, with heron's gait,
you stalk yourself from

shadow. To brace you, we
must let you be. To break

you, shake you, and you'll
puke. Whole, when all is

said, you're 'rabbit-bold',
a joke. Christopher, you

are nervy, head-sick,
wire-limbed, pervy.

IV *Christ*

Psychohistorically, we
believe a pictured He

would match with our man
Hurleigh – ectomorph

and surly, with slight
gynandromorphy – girly.

Diagnosis – neurosis:
performance impaired

through sense of
impending disaster.

Apocryphal

Like butter on water, a tic on the skin
of the lake where it bobs. A limb on a hook,
hauled in by men. A leg with a shoe, with a name.

It is beached and observed: like a fish,
a luminous grey. Unshoe it, unsock it, return
it to town in a truck. Human remains.

Get it a docket. Call in the weeping, who will
bicker like birds at the side of the coffin:
which end to put it. The place of the ruff.

Bury it. Bury it. Dig a hole like a dog does,
then pray like a man, for a man. Leave flowers,
forget it for years, till the day when you're

told of a man who returns to the site
of the grave and a locket of water. Laughter.
A man on a crutch, with a shoe, with that name.

*

I am watching you work. Your eyes wide like
asterisks on the page of your face. You are
reading a book, you say, which poses a question

you cannot unhook. Look, I am quoting: *Someone
is crossing the bridge. But is it me?* You are
scowling, and curling your lip like a line

which is cast to the drowning. No wonder,
at night, you are lifting the covers to see
for yourself what you're like: a sack-full,

a mind-full, a heat and a sweat, the tattoo
of a heart which is yours. You are reading:
If you lost your mind. would you know it?

Life Model

1 *Like Schiele*

Look – up and tangle
the flexion of shanks,

the dapple my hand
rakes, my hair, the air

the light is passing
through to blood

that cools and plots
its course.

This skin's
a thermogram they read

from: ochre, jade
and puce. To pull,

to hook myself in space –
akimbo, wanting, I

lack the charge. Turn
down the dwelling eye.

2 *Like Matisse*

Just as I have thought myself
into the travelling blank,
blue line, that smooth
electric shade, some bastard

in the collage-workshop
pastes on newsprint where
my head must go – *VACANCIES*
he reads, progresses *WOMEN*

on my heart, then hazards
roughly *BRIEFLY* on each breast,
across my cunt rips *SPORT*.
Puts *BUSINESS* on my arse.

3 *Like Freud*

On the face of it, the pearl-boned, angled
hip's no more than a body's easy warp,
a natured languor, posed indifference
in a waxy daylight. Her umbered arm
might dangle, dally on a crumpled sheet
for hours, as though she were alone. As if
the buckled, crooked leg did not occlude
the glare, throw shadow where her legs fork. Cut

under this a knowledge of my nerve-wracked,
knuckled torso, the blood-full yoke of muscle
which binds my neck, my face away from where
a brush-tip's kiss might blight my open eyes.

4 *Like Sherman*

*That dream you have, the one where you're naked, and lying
stretched out in the back of your car, embarrassed but bold
as your friend takes the wheel. Are you drunk? You remember,
you think, just passing a woman, a suitcase and lake
where you stop for a beer at the bar and she's staring –
the woman – in close-up – in colour. She speaks as she
looks but all you can think of is hiding, and phoning
your wife, who is waiting. Waiting for change, you kill
the jump-cut, freeze-frame image you have of her laughing,
return to the bar where she's sitting to eat. You eat,
but the food is disgusting, decaying – she's making
a scene: she's crawling, you're crawling, the floor is dirt
where you're digging. You're naked. I am wearing that dream.*

The Vanishing Point

Human Beings like you are very rare in the world. You act as a prism.
You are Sagawa, who ate a human being.
INTERVIEWER TO ISSEI SAGAWA,
WHO KILLED AND ATE HIS GIRLFRIEND

I *Framed*

On the ground were the two bodies, entwined
and, presently, still... Listen. This is what

you expect; there are two ways of seeing
things. 1. *On the ground were the two bodies,*

entwined and, presently, still. His eyes shut
as if to kiss, his mouth was fast against

the mouth... See? The radio is talking
dirty... *his mouth was fast against the mouth...*

But listen. 2. (This is not what you think...)
...against the mouth of the wound... You want me

to continue?... *the wound where the bullet*
had entered her body... Then you come to

the eyewitness... *where her head had been was*
framed with blood, like... rupturing the speaker.

14

II *You are Sagawa*

You are Sagawa, who ate a human being
Sagawa, whose voice is a hawkmoth.

You are Sagawa, who ate a human being
Sagawa. Small. Sphagnum-tongued.

Sagawa, who ate a human being?
Shithead. Meatbrain. Sagawa.

You are Sagawa
Fish-gilled, breathing blood.

Sagawa, you ate a human being
Sagawa dreaming. Waking.

Sagawa

Mother and father of appetites, I am
Sagawa, who'll kiss you, for starters.

Who acts as a prism?
Sagawa the hammer, the pane of glass.

It will be as the light • wings across you •
there will be • a woman • water flowing •
into water • intimate as water •
appetent and eye • for you are touching •
the world with your skin • strange and ablaze she •
will be held • gently so gently • you will •
weep sweet come • in the sweet palm of your hand •

It will be. As the light wings across you,
there will be a woman, water flowing
into water, intimate as water.
Appetent and eye, for you are touching
the world. With your skin strange and ablaze, she
will be held gently. So gently you will
weep. Sweet come in the sweet palm of your hand.

2351 hrs. (APPLAUSE) *Good evening Issei Sagawa!*
2352 hrs. Check out the idiot boards.
2353 hrs. Walk across the floor of the TV studio.
2354 hrs. Answer the question about taste. (APPLAUSE)
2355 hrs. The host appeals for a volunteer, a woman.
2356 hrs. *Issei Sagawa...* the host says ... *what do you think*
2357 hrs. *of the girl we have here for you?* (APPLAUSE)
2358 hrs. *Oh*, I say, *I love big girls.* Then leaning forward
2359 hrs. like an uncle to touch her cheek, I say
0000 hrs. *You are so nice I could eat you.* (EXIT/LAUGHS)

Goodbye Jones

The noise of the fist will be
the noise of the door, next.

Next to that, the news
on a postcard. A hundred words.

In England, you have found
the perfect flyover... *Near*

Bristol... you write, having
parked the Reliant Robin

by the transport caff and gorge,
spending your last on chips.

You decide: *Today, I'm
ditching gravity. Wish me*

luck... losing your skirts
for the first ascent

to carve your name in stone.
A fortnight later, postmarked

Portugal, a polaroid arrives.
You bless the man, weather,

and sweat you've found,
build houses in the sand.

I am finding myself...
Liar, Jones. Call me...

Thankyou, thankyou, thankyou.

Speaking for Jones

1 *Jones's Husband*

Fretwork. Found
thing. A stray. I

took Jones in. On
like a puzzle. She

moved in with nothing
but trouble, and would wait

like a cat with a grin
for me to come home. To

be honest, I ditched
her because of her

drivel: the dribble
of tears. That evening

I straightened her
out. Uncurled her. I

opened her up. Not
what you'd think:

she was stiff with
a giggle. A joke. I

screwed her back up,
like a rag. In my

hands.

2 Jones's Wife

Through bad luck, I lost
Jones in the traffic.

Jones ... I said ... *we*
must ... but never finished,

as Jones sped off, leaving
the head I'd leant

towards the open window
bobbing into space,

I felt. Jones
had always known

that one day the car
would join the others

on the road. Jones felt
this was the system.

I loved Jones, and Jones
loved me. When I think

of earth, I think
of Jones. Of air –

I think of Jones out
there in sun and dust.

Moving.

3 *Jones's Dog*

Yet moving, Jones
is the still point

around which I run.
I am alone

in this perception.
Also, Jones, any time,

can be a chair.
In support, I say

that Jones is soft.
There have been times,

Jones shared my floor
and times I've sat

at Jones's table.
Jones will sing

while walking,
as my ears know.

Finally, I'd like to say
that in the meantime,

Jones can be called upon
to make good smells.

Tenderly.

Smith Quizzes Jones

SMITH: What is your idea of perfect happiness?

JONES: *I am watching myself on a screen in the dark,*
at home, alone, and I'm miming or mocking the frame
as I see it. I'm lost in this. Then, hiatus, I
laugh as it jams, as my mouth becomes black. Turns to white.

SMITH: What do you think is your greatest extravagance?

JONES: *I am naming and numbering the hairs on my head*
and counting each breath; the becoming of sky in my blood.
I'm saving the dirt I wash from my skin, and I'm
trapping the rain in my cells, the rain in my cup.

SMITH: What objects do you carry with you at all times?

JONES: *Nil, Smith. Zero. Not a book nor a key, a lock*
nor a drug. Not a dream that recurs to marble my
mind – no birthmark. No thing, but a sense of the tick-tack
of clouds; the scar of the sun in a tidemark of light.

SMITH: How would you like to die?

(Jones refuses this question.)

SMITH: How would you like to die?

JONES: *As I was saying: when the film stops and my mouth*
becomes ash, then my face, my head, like an opening
eye, I switch off the machine and I sit in the dark –
drawn in like a fist or a frown. A question. Full stop.

SMITH: What one thing would improve your quality of life?

JONES: *I am building a house that has twenty-six rooms.*
I am marking the door to each room with a cypher.
I am arranging my things according to letter.
Then I'll lock up and leave it, forget it. Erasure.

SMITH: What would your motto be?

JONES: *That the quick brown fox jumps over the lazy dog.*

Jones in the Kitchen, Jones on the Lawn

Might I faint? I
think from laughing –
makes me dark.

In this domestic
interior, Jones
finds Jones, a box,

a vase of stems.
The pot and flame.
Film-maker, square

the view in which
I am in front, behind,
making a shape

for myself, of myself.
I say... Jones
in the kitchen, Jones

on the lawn: bending
and kneeling – hearing –
ear to the ground.

Jones's Best Joke

Q: What's brown and sticky?
A: A stick.

* * *

Symmetry

True – it was always evening when she called,
passing *The Prospect of Whitby*, the changing

lights and skyline of what was going down,
or going up. The spice wharf drew a trace,

a map, a story which her senses knew by heart
and followed. She liked the boy, the warehouse

buttressing the Thames, the water which absorbed
but not reflected light. She held on steady,

trusted the street's amnesia, fucked the father.
It was always evening. When she called,

the boy was dressed in leather, was introducing
friends still sleeping on the sofa, had stuck

a mirror shattered in the fight like crazy paving
on the wall. She liked him there spreadeagled,

joyriding his broken image. For her, it was the crux.
Thus cruciform, benighted, he was glad and leapt

to turn his studded heel on tattered boards. She
felt that, felt her own amnesia, fucked the son.

Time and Again

Wild Time

Where one in otherwise *summer*
time was tipped earthwards,

down but with two long
shins and a hand skywards,

in that tunnelly moment
called falling. Noticing

then the shiny scene
wherein 'I' was mostly

what was never seen:
from here, suppose a fly.

The grass, then, millions
and taller. The sky,

a thousand spinning
blues. Up there, upended

limbs are ends of me, I
wriggle out and back

to vertical.
Knees and push.

Play Time

Back then, the ashy
muffle of 'back then'.

Outwit, and lurch
to tarmac and a pack

to run both with
and from. Nip down

my size to half –
the world's all

looming. I and others
get the hang and grow.

And witness what we
do through dodge

and drop, how
the faces of us

knot the duffled
view with crabbing

hands of each. We
pass and rise.

Tea Time

Tick. Click. Real-time's
the tilt on this bit

as the manner's pastel
in an English dream. Yet,

the lip to lip of cup
to me is causing

a rim's white crescent
which I'm dull behind

and dulling, as the angle's
on the vapid *proper*

facts and tact we crunch.
The space of me's

a soft beat, a pitch
by which to pace

the dip or bob
of glottis, the swallowed

hours, or ends of
speak and spit.

Bed Time

Is full of eye, sheer
you, all shoulder, cheek,

and neck to lip. The tip
of now's a burst –

the day's becoming
strobe, an absence,

pulse of shadows.
The growing shown

is grey, the silver
hand, the web and wall

above now sharper. You
will fall quiet, then,

the day itself has breath,
will murmur dreamlike

as the trees find green,
the houses form, and windows

light. We have
begun and turned.

Tap

There are even silences, prosecutors
of the auricle to bring charges
against bunched cartilage. Here,

we are the captives of the peripheral
nerves. Cauliflower, jug or shell-like
conjoin with the mechanical synapse,

a telephone flyblown with voices –
Grapevine, Talkabout, Chatline.
3 a.m. and the plastic is pressed

to the lobe, mole-like. Tones dust
the inner drum like a moth glass-trapped.
Hearsay. Static. Molecules become

alphabets and into ear, malleus
and incus at it like Punch's truncheon,
hammering and hammering

the cochlea, coiled and recoiled.
The tongue upstarts – jumps
and flicks each outbreathed breath

to word: unleashing a thesaurus.
What is moot is *polyglot,
medley. Babel 61 n. confusion.*

The You Sign Poems

You Sign 1

you sign: we
don't hear
like you
high sound

makes
my cheekbones
hum
my skull

can sense
high sounds
most sounds
I feel

in my
bones
my sternum
ribcage

diaphragm
very low
down
my pelvis

feels
the bass
the bass
is genital

You Sign 2

you sign: when
she shouted
at me
shouted

I felt
drops of spittle
speckle
my face like

pins and needles
I saw
her face
go dog

I signed:
Dog-face
always let
your top lip

know
what your
bottom lip
is doing

You Sign 3

you sign:
two butterflies
dancing
tarantellas

outside
the window
reminded me
of children's hands

telling
different
stories
to their

lips
like inchworms
arching oh
oh sorry

it broke
in my
hands
like eggshell

You Sign 4

you sign:
boxers
are bilingual
one minute

they pug
the air
like cats
give

false directions
left right
then
right left

their gloves
will not
translate
on impact

KO's OK
then the word
is nonce
out for the count

You Sign 5

You sign: I
had difficulty
imagining
schizophrenia

until
I saw
my friend's
reflections

in the glass
so many
hands like
many birds

many signs
I could not
catch
the drift

of signs
could not
ignore
the birds

You Sign 6

you sign: when
I want her
to know
I love her

I put
my mouth
next to
her ear

my tongue
gently
feathers
her skin

with words
my tongue
her ear
no lies

Drive

1 *Simply Said*

His simple is
in how a spider does

in air, work, but
leaving no stickier

trace – that is,
not even to catch

the metaphorical
fly – will *will*

the uprush of
his hourly idea,

(the one he's certain
of and dreaming),

until his tongue
clucks *You...*,

the work of it
delight and luck,

for this is Billy
talking with his heart,

saying
You. Blue car. Drive!

2 *Said So*

It was under him then, the tar lick
with its slip of miles. Too, the looped
hour, the only map he knew. To this

becoming light was where, as morning
greased it all, he went, followed
the coast road to a pebbled stop

and water, the butt of cool air
shining in his lungs What colour is
it? *Peacock*, the day it is? *Tomorrow*.

3 *Says Who?*

Let's say I'm in the quiet bar, as usual,
thinking the usual nothing, and the beer,

if you like, is amber. The light is, too.
Well. What happens is, I want to do

what he does: want to play the monkey
with the eye I've caught, mirror that

sad/stupid/ happy face – show I've learnt
the language for it: body language for cabbage.

4 *Sooth*

If ever
this unrolling,
reeling, handsprung,
wave

or man
did go, *did*
or could leave
mark – you

might say
it was in that
hard black
pebble,

the eye
of anemone, or
fingerprints
of starfish;

in the way
you thought
a man had somehow
touched

and claimed
the dark rock
at the bottom of
the pool.

Says Are Meant
(for Liban)

Plot by boy, day, as he steps
in boots and reaches
from his bed for seeing what
and says, first thing *I dream.*

He does, but tethers now
to strides he makes, and hoofs
to play, not like a horse,
but more – to say the air

will itch, is true. Whatever
holds him, holds him just
for seconds. Say he's
crouching, naked, four,

and bridling know for purpose
of, for purpose of explaining
how it's broken – cracks
he's found, he says are meant.

Person on the Line

North. Midsummer. This service terminates
here. Imagine holding your breath
as the brakes scream. Release it.
We're getting there. The message burns
along the journey's lit fuse...

We apologise for the late...
Drop ideas like leaves, like ice.
A landscape softens, disappears.
An incident. The arrival of this train.
Circumstances beyond our control.

Imagine that. Don't imagine that.

Inmates

The boy yell, bull elephant charge
of sound: a dead-pan sift of noise
through the ward to staff quarters.

Caroline's having a fit in perfect treble:
butterfly convulsions. She propels herself
like wind-up Donald Duck capsized.

I'm going to HANG *myself,* says Mark,
but temporarily is satisfied with
stretching his neck as far

as it will go up the chimney. Lying
crucified in the grate, his trousers
stain with the thrill of extension.

Sitting together during Recreation,
she concentrates, shifts her tits
nervously inside a cheap print dress

like a female impersonator at the
Rotary Club party. He pats his breast
pocket – inside lie six inches of string:

a tight possibility balled against
his heart. They discuss whether it's enough,
whether you could hang on so much.

Seq

1 *Was*

Inescapable: to start with the history
of a place or a thing, people – circumstances.

Take, for instance, the way a shadow's hinged,
how it meets a wall, stands upright less than a person is.

I suppose the was of it – of them – was what
I overheard, a half-shadow or, perhaps,

the story like a swimmer seen from somewhere up;
a surface and a kick or flap, then gone. She was

saying how she'd found herself that day (they weren't
speaking) before the mirror – God knows how –

with one hand pleasuring herself. But what of her other
hand? She'd seen it scribbling the glass,

her features uglied to grimace, all *cock-eyed*,
she said, *like he was, over me*. She came.

2 *Is*

In her absence, he
acts strangely. He is frisking
the space where she was.

Holding a pubic
hair between thumb and forefinger;
retractable vice.

A detective! No.
A shaman; he eats the hair,
he sees her image.

3 *Ago*

All night they had watched the slow
arc of a star, a satellite's
tracing of the galaxy.

On earth, the unthinkable: he'd lost
his mind. He sensed it falling past him
like sycamore seeds as he made love

to her. She opened her eyes just as he
pulled his face awry: they came
together, naked, resembling each other.

4 *Meanwhile*

Dog-eared, genial, days pad through the house
following a sinew of fragrance. Full
now the memory needs no flowers, twines
of clematis; what is anoints itself.
Passing and becoming annihilate
the world. Look, a toy train shuttles away
from the valley; an insect balances
on the wine's meniscus; a cat cyphers
contentment on the windowsill. Measured
like this it's a time of perpetual ease,
snapshot, moment of grace or gracelessness.
A touch insinuates such radiance
and pulls away. There's no need for others.
Overheard. A half-shadow. Or. Perhaps.

The Bone Die

Even the wrist's fast jack
is funked by a thumb's rub,

chances and freaked odds
of plane, pit, dot and dot

are pocketed or scuttled:
a weathered die contrives

its craft of luck from years –
edges all unwhet, or honed

in captivities of palm. Thrown
down hard for a free run (an ack ack

clatter after gulling) it's pulling
up dead on a rising surface

and jinxes still by a worn slant:
two up, two up, where fractures web

the sockets of its eyes – askance –
laugh lines – a probability of chaos.

Making Conversation

1 *Gesture*

Queer the way
the mouth let slip

the whether
or not of how

it might begin.
Rum the pantomime

of lips, the labial
shrug through which

the unspeakable
air was forced. Odd

the glottal break
kicking the throat

and busy the hands
and turned the back.

Queer the noise
and queer the pitch.

NOTE: The nicknames *Gesture*, *Bow Wow*, *Yo He Ho*,
Ding Dong, *Pooh Pooh* and *Musical* all describe actual
theories of the origin of speech.

2 *Bow Wow*

The pitch not
of a lark, more

like bull – a bubble
of it, bellow. Below

the normal scale
but rising after

nap, cat nap.
Actually, barking.

Baulked at more
than merely

mewling, moaning –
oh dear, this

time groaning,
horsing, aping

all the zoo, and
tired. Dog-tired.

3 *Yo He Ho*

Dog-tired from this
huf puf seith that

and all the haul.
Pulling out the stops

say that it heave
our heart

for help and handy,
timely assistance

please. Look at
one – toil, another –

moil. Well together
we think we

work. We think
'Like Trojans' and

to think we thought
to say it. Hey!

4 *Ding Dong*

'Hay' was what
came to me as I cut

through it,
suddenly aware as I

stalked through
it that was

clearly field – and
sown, grown, mown –

you name it. Then,
philosophically,

you understand, I
understood, you

must be sure to name
the thing you know,

and if you don't know
it, no it, you know.

5 *Pooh Pooh*

No! Not 'field'
but felt. The first

stir of it needful,
hearty, hate or

angry shake to
clear the throat

and tongue of
something, something

clotting. And then
there is escape,

the hiss and built
pressure which

is felt, the feeling
raw. The roar

of this has bloomed
like light or flower.

6 *Musical*

Flower gave us choice:
convolvulus or heartsease?

Picked, I think
the second. For sound

and sentiment.
And song we did

then, mostly
to each other, but

with joy, we were
appealing, keening,

harking our utmost –
eyeing, concealing

nothing amid all.
Still it goes on,

from lilt, swing, trill,
bop, blues to hum.

Diary of Eleni Altamura 1821–1900

1 *From Athens with Yannis & Sophia*

Black cowled at daybreak
they crouch at the strike
of the sea's haunch,
count omens of dolphins.
From their throats grief
surfaces and spumes:
a witchery of stoops
is the craft's rocking.

This far, I have travelled
with them, sourness hacked
on the black cloth of my breast
as our returning ends.
Towards us tides Spetsai –
involute on lighted water.
I have hope, an impulse thriving
through the ocean's muscle.

Eleni Altamura worked as an artist in Athens until she
returned to Spetsai with her children who were dying
of TB. After they died, she burned all her existing
canvases and remained mute for the rest of her life.

2 *At Kounoupitsa*

A white dog skitters
into a sandsquall.
On the Dapia, fishermen
fold nets like winding-sheets,
folk gather for a day's barter.
I buy food enough for feasting:
there is a whispering –
Eleni's children are dying.

Outside Kounoupitsa, hooves
cleave hot, on cobbles –
Ella! Ella! – Quickly!
is the horsemen's taunt.
Traced from limit to limit
of the sun's arching,
I am made ancient
by the cicada's tedium.

3 *Burn*

It all. A drift of almond,
orange oil and ash. A net
of embers grips the yard
as others shout and spider
out of smoke, from fire.
What roots is grief,
through heat. A prayer
of earth-oil. Mud gag.

To burn it all. Inside,
the house is deep
with wishes, flowers,
and the thousand eyes
of times – black garlands
of belonging. Adrift
in crimson, son and daughter,
dust and white. Gone.

4 *After Burial at Aghia Anna*

I began at dusk, before
the weak light of shrines
chafed and mocked the bruised
blue of falling dark.
Working up a slurry of dirt,
my hands like spades –
I felt the ground was warm,
I could hear breathing.

I used the axe. I think
I was crying, either
that or it was the sound
of pinewood splitting.
When they dragged me off,
a white lizard darted
onto the box, tongue-tip
threading air, stitching silence.

Environment

1 *Elsewhere*

Having arrived, the first
and last thing you

acquire is a taste
for absolutes: as if

you have become
a part of the slip-meet

at the fell's foot,
scratchings, and Hush.

Water travels elsewhere,
under-running Dowgang

and Redwing, leaving
a clench of rust

on rubble. You note
the dead roots, forests

shifting slowly out
of kilter and into

other. Whatever leaves,
returns, or stays

the eye is wile:
tail-flick or leaf-fall,

to harry, pass or dream
time. This dispossession.

2 *Hoardings*

So so-so, this accumulation
of odds and ends, refuse

the digger will bank into
skips. The dog – days

hungry – knows the nub
of the matter is being

able to minnow the gap
between concrete and wire,

make off through the no-go,
past metal, metal and blinding,

to become made dust:
cumulonimbus rising

out of the dip of the track.
Out of the dip of the track,

the horizon is visible:
rooftops, cables, chimneys

you would hammer down
like tacks, people

grouped under the hoardings;
ads for bitter or multiscreen:

The Final Nightmare, For the Boys,
Die Hard, Truly, Madly, Deeply.

3 *Provincial*

Here, and here again
through the region's

knap and sink
of anywhere, seen

from any window:
this door, that street –

not, but not
far from the diktat

of knack, of knowing that
where the weather is *fine*

the people are also
without astonishment

at birdsong, or the memory
of it, the migrant

nuance of alarm,
to which, in the gardens,

the municipal tulip
is anathema, emblem

of radical boredom.
Here, and here again.

You know, gan be gyp
to the ditto, if doggo.

Dr Roget's Bedside Manner

*Peter Mark Roget worked as a doctor. He compiled his
'thesaurus' because he felt that by widening his vocabulary,
he would be better able to communicate with his students.*

I *Abstract Relations*

Odd pawk this that's
laid her up for good:

copper helix like a
fiddlehead's lovelock

in her womb. The aborted
little tiny, future

bantling's all in driblets;
limb from limb and

bit by bit.
Semi, hemi, aliquot.

II *Space*

Abysm, from which there
is an exodus of keck and

gurk, and pardon, ouch,
excuse me. This one's

really shotten herring:
feed with skilly, brewis

brose. Until tomorrow,
collywobbly. Operation

pending.
P.S. Appendix.

III *Matter*

Doomed. There is a point
at which the pap appears

to reach its critical
mass. When it comes to

the push: agues, grief.
The word is *cancer*.

There is no hope:
the patient's now *in*

articulo mortis, swansong:
crunk, pule, pip. Croak.

IV *Intellect*

Idioglossia, so to speak,
is blether and blat. Tics:

multi- and poly-. Politic
to isolate – not, to wit,

to woo disaster through
folie à deux. Look out!

Incarcerate the madman,
in bedlam, the bin; he'll

hornswoggle, clack –
queer fish – ad infinitum.

V *Volition*

About as independent
as a hog on ice. His

last days were a
shilly-shally between

going and staying.
What it came down to

was a rope, a chair.
Lesions. Post Mortem.

Result of action:
suicide, a lesser evil.

VI *Affections*

Sob-stuff, you think?
Well, I knew this rip,

got his comeuppance;
too much moll and mopsy

I'd guess, or demi-rep.
Debagged, putrescent,

in my office, I told
him *syphilis*. Expect

fistula. Ooze.
Ultimately, loss of face.